MW01286145

# ME

# MYSELF

# &

# I

# THE UNHOLY TRINITY

## Romel Duane Moore Sr.

## Prayer Changes Things Publishing

Prayer Changes Things (PCT) Publishing
7551 Kingsport Road
Indianapolis, Indiana  46256

Scripture quotations, unless otherwise noted are from the King James Version of the Bible.

Cover design by Jan Taylor

Printed in the United States of America.

Edited by Fiverr Mary450

ISBN-13: 978-1539602538
ISBN-10: 1539602532

The name satan is intentionally not capitalized.

# CONTENTS

# DEDICATION

This book is dedicated to my friend George Eldridge Jr. and his wife Phyllis of twenty-eight years.  Thank you for telling me the truth even when it hurts and being there for me whenever I needed you. Proverbs 17:17 says, *"A friend loves at all times and a brother is born for adversity."*

# INTRODUCTION

A certain man noticed that the hummingbird taking up residence in the birdhouse in his front yard began to fly violently into his car after he would return home. After realizing it was not an isolated incident, he began to pay closer attention to the bird's behavior. He noticed the bird would fly violently into the car, but not just any part of the vehicle, but particularly, only the mirrors, glass, and chrome parts. He did a little research about hummingbirds and discovered that they are very territorial and will defend their turf with great zeal. This led him to understand that the hummingbird was not going crazy each time it crashed into his car, but because it only flew into the parts of the car that gave a clear reflection, the bird actually thought he was engaging the enemy, when in reality, who he thought was the enemy was really himself.

The hummingbird did not understand that he was the enemy and that is why he continued to fly violently into the car. Usually, what we see in others who infuriate us and cause us to become angry, judgmental, and even violent, is just a reflection of what is actually on the inside of us. Instead of pointing the finger, or slandering others, we need to take a "checkup from the neck up" and make sure we are not like the hummingbird: quick to defend unauthorized territory and perpetuating repeated mistakes, accidents, and head-on collisions. What this story reveals to us is that the real enemy is exactly that: IN-A-ME.

Jesus explained to us that when we see a speck in our brother's eye, we have a plank in our own eye. Before we can help cure the speck in our brother's eye, we must first remove the plank from our eye (*Matthew 7:3-5*). This is a task very few of us take seriously and really do something about. However, if we want to avoid the pain and embarrassment of what the hummingbird went through, wisdom tells us to look in the mirror for our faults, before we look at our neighbor's faults.

The only person we can change is ourselves. Yet ninety-nine percent of our time and effort is spent attempting to change others. Like it or not, what happens to us in life, we are the only ones who can change anything. As an individual, you alone are the only one who can change your behavior. Regardless of your color, gender, or religion and regardless of the injustices that may have occurred to you because of your color, gender, or religion, there is a universal law that is constant: no one can do yourself more harm than yourself. We are our greatest enemy. Until we face this truth and work on changing ourselves, we will remain powerless and go through life always accusing someone else for our failures, shortcomings, and character flaws.

# CHAPTER 1

## *In-A-Me*

I was the most stuck up, arrogant person you'd ever meet, and I didn't have a clue I was that way. I came out of the womb an introvert who just wanted to be left alone. I didn't desire anyone's attention or affirmation. I was at peace in my skin and didn't understand why people were drawn to me. I was the firstborn and didn't have other siblings for a few years. Adults were always on my face pinching or kissing my fat jaws and stating how cute I was. I hated the attention. I always had a serious demeanor, and most times if you violated my personal space, I made sure you knew it. I was called mean more times than I can remember. I didn't see the evidence of pride because I never desired others attention, but pride was there nonetheless. As I grew up, I kept to myself. In school, if you didn't see me you wouldn't have known I was in class because I barely spoke. I was always the shortest person in the class. I didn't begin to grow until I hit high school so on top of my introverted personality, I had a chip on my shoulder. This was not a good combination! Upon meeting me, I was no less than rude and disrespectful. People would approach me stating how handsome I was, but with a face that looked like a pitbull dipped in lemonade, I wouldn't even respond. Others would approach me and politely say, smile; it's going to be ok. Those type of statements made my blood boil. With every available facial muscle, I would squint and frown even harder to show you how stupid a statement that was. It wasn't that I was unhappy. I simply did not warrant outside interference.

Never once did I see the pride in my life because I knew I cared less what others thought about me and didn't crave their attention. Once I gave my heart to Christ and seriously got into God's Word, He began to show me myself. Around the age of twenty-three, I was praying, and the Lord spoke to me and said I was full of pride. I wholeheartedly responded with confusion and asked how? The Lord said I've always received compliments, affirmation, and attention, but never gave it to others. It was a simple case of deposits and withdrawals. I instantly understood what He meant. Whether I desired others affirmation or not, I received it, and my storehouse was running over, but the amount of affirmation, compliments, and attention I gave others was worse than anemic. This revelation humbled me. God did not beat me up for being a hermit by nature because that was the way I was made, but He gently spoke truth to my heart that changed the course of my life. Some people naturally see the best in others and have the personality to give congratulations and praise, while others, like myself, who by nature are bashful, find it extremely difficult to hold a conversation let alone give others accolades. I've spent most of my life wishing I were as gregarious as others I know, but that is not me. The Holy Spirit has slowly taught me how to come out of my shell and engage with others and allow them into my world. More importantly, He has changed my heart to be able to see others gifts, and worth, and speak into their lives.

I'm sure you know someone whose standoffish personality may rub you the wrong way. It does not mean they have a negative spirit about them. It could be they are simply bashful and have not learned how to comingle effectively with others. We are all under construction and have light years to go in our development. Many of us struggle with the simplest things in life while others may seem to conquer the world. We can't judge a book by its cover. Only God knows the whole story.

## CHAPTER TWO

---

## *Daddy*

---

My mother had me at a young age. She was a beautiful woman, mentally and emotionally strong and accepted her responsibility of this fat jawed, high yellow, screaming and hollering baby boy. I cried so much that I put my fingers in my ears so I wouldn't have to hear myself. My biological father was around when I was born, but I was too young to remember his face. I grew up in Chicago and never received an invitation from him to meet. My mother's family was pretty big, and he always knew someone he could get in touch with if he desired to connect with me. I never received an invitation. A lot of my pride I got from my mother. It has never crossed my mind to go searching for my biological father because I always had a father; my stepfather.

My stepfather was a man of the streets. Like my mother, he grew up in the urban landscape of Chicago with the unique Chicago culture that goes along with it. He was a hustler. Someone who could shoot pool to pay the bills. One of the things he did teach me was how to box. I come up in the era of Muhammad Ali, Sugar Ray Leonard, Tommy Hitman Hearns and Marvelous Marvin Hagler. What I call the golden age of boxing. This was before the use of guns on the streets got out of control. In my day, the man you fought toe to toe usually became your best friend. My stepfather reminds me of a scene from the movie Gladiator where the dying Emperor's son, Commodus, told his father his personal qualities after the Emperor told him he would not take his place as Emperor. Commodus stated:

*"You wrote to me once, listing the fourteen virtues. Wisdom, justice, fortitude, and temperance. As I read the list, I knew I had none of them. But I have other virtues, father. Ambition. That can be a virtue when it drives us to excel. Resourcefulness. Courage. Perhaps not on the battlefield, but there are many forms of courage.*

*Devotion. To my family. To you. But none of my virtues were on your list."*

My stepfather may not have possessed everything we typically looked for in a husband and father, but like Commodus, he possessed other virtues. Resourcefulness, courage, and loyalty. I did not see it then, but he gave us everything he had within him to give. Too many times we are looking for qualities in others that we might desperately need and want, but they do not possess to give us. People simply cannot give what they do not have. He was an alcoholic and substance abuser. He struggled keeping jobs and because of his addictions, many times did not bring his wages home. On the other hand, he had a great personality and loved to host get-togethers for family and friends. He could sing and loved music. My passion for music today came from his influence. I recognize today how opposite our personalities were and how my introverted ways, smart mouth, and attitude problem must have gotten under his skin every time he saw me. I could give you one look that said more about how I felt about you than a fifty-page essay.

I spent my entire high school years depressed and looking for any way out from under him. It felt like there wasn't a day that went past where we did not bump heads. As the man of the house he was not going to back down and as a young, pompous, self-righteous jerk, I was not giving up any ground. There would be no compromise. I ended up being emancipated at the age of sixteen and moving out the house. I was eager and ready to be my own man in this world. I dreamed of being married with two little boys to raise and mold into great men.

I entered into manhood broken and depressed. I didn't understand that a problem unlearned is a problem returned and all the daddy issues hidden in my heart weren't going to disappear magically. I got married at the age of seventeen. I was married that morning and graduated from high school that evening. You could not tell me that I wasn't making the right decision. My uncompromising pride would not have allowed you to show me how horrible an idea this was and how no matter how intelligent and mature I thought I might have been, that we were in no way ready for the weight and responsibility of love, marriage and family at my age.

Anyone who knew me knew I was too bullheaded and arrogant to do anything other than what I desired.

*Restoration*

I lived in a home with a mother and father and two other siblings. Even though we lived in the same home in many ways I felt like the outcast. I was much lighter than my brothers and stepfather. In spite of excelling academically and athletically, something deep inside me was never at peace. When I later read the scripture that said a bastard shall not enter the temple, I immediately understood on some level the intended ramifications. Though God forgives any and all sins when we come to Him and repent, but there are many heart issues we need to be healed from that will only occur after establishing an intimate relationship with the Holy Ghost. The Cross deals with our sins, but the Holy Ghost deals with the sinner. Passover is for the sins and Pentecost is for the person who has sin problems. My hidden struggle with peace would not be resolved until after I gave my heart to Christ and established a genuine relationship with God's Spirit who then opens the Word of God to me specifically to deal with my daddy issues.

## Call no man father

Around the age of twenty-three, the Spirit of God began performing open heart surgery on me. He'd wake me in the middle of the night to show me intimate things in the Bible to heal the areas that plagued my heart for so long. The Lord knew I suffered from rejection concerning father in my life. He knew for me to be the best father I could be for my sons I needed to be delivered from the agony of my father's rejection. One of my greatest fears as a young man of God was experiencing the rejection of my spiritual leader. I had tasted its bitterness on every level except from a spiritual leader, and the thought and fear stayed tucked away in my heart. God was not having it anymore and systematically walked me through scripture and revealed to me the great importance of a father's affirmation to his children, especially the sons.  The Spirit of God highlighted areas of the life of David to me.  He revealed to me David's rejection from Saul after he killed the giant Goliath and the many years of Saul's attempts to assassinate David.  David was summoned from his own father's house to serve under King Saul at a young age.  Saul served as a father figure to David in many ways, yet that role model continually attempted to take his life.  Reading David's unfortunate plight with Saul really ministered to me.  I related to the father, son narrative of David and Saul.  In many areas I felt like David.  I understood how it felt to be picked out to be picked on by a father figure.  Though I was to blame concerning much of the conflict with my stepfather, at this stage in my life I did not see and understand it and still needed to be healed from the experiences I did have.  The example I saw in David's life was how he chased after God while Saul chased after him.  When we chase after God, He will not leave us comfortless.  God gave David opportunities to get revenge with Saul and each time David refuse to capitalize on it and walked away without harming Saul.  This is where we got the coined phrase, *"touch not God's anointed and do His prophets no harm."* Times presented itself to me where I could have retaliated and really hurt my stepfather, but because of the honorable example I learned from reading about David, I chose not to.

---

*Jesus needed affirmation*

---

The Holy Ghost continued to walk me through scripture showing me strained father-son relationships, and I saw myself in each story and felt me gaining my footing with each story. Finally, The Spirit took me to the life of Jesus. Understanding Jesus is one hundred percent man and one hundred percent God. We don't know at what age He lost his earthly father, Joseph. We know Joseph was still alive at Jesus age of twelve. At some point, Jesus experienced the loss of his earthly father. Joseph never got the opportunity to see Jesus become the Messiah. We don't know if Jesus ever heard Joseph tell him that he loved him. What we do know is that before Jesus was incarnate through the womb of the Virgin Mary that He is the second Person of the Trinity and had no beginning and had always been in the bosom of the Father. Coming to Earth in the form of man has implications that we will never be able to understand as Jesus left His splendor and glory and became like you and I. The Spirit took me to the Baptism of Christ and opened my eyes. After Jesus came up out of the water from John the Baptist baptizing Him, it states the heavens were opened, and God spoke audibly stating, *"This is my beloved Son in whom I am well pleased."* When I read these words from God, I began to weep. It instantly spoke to my innermost being. I automatically understood that God didn't speak audibly from Heaven for the bystanders to hear, but He understood as a man, Jesus needed to hear and know that His father loved Him. Jesus heard His Heavenly Father say, *"This is my beloved son in whom I am well pleased."* Even Jesus needed His Father's affirmation. At that moment I was healed, and I felt all the layers and years of rejection of being rejected by my biological father and drama and rejection of my stepfather lift right off my broken heart. Jesus is truly touched by the feelings of our infirmities. Understanding that the King of kings and Lord of lords needed to hear His Father accept and affirm Him meant the world to me. Much of the sorrow we experience comes from feeling alone in our tribulation. My mother always used to greet me with *"my beloved son in whom I am well pleased."* I appreciated her words and loved her deeply for going out of her way to express it to me, but it wasn't her love and affirmation that I lacked. Nothing can replace the love of fathers. God placed it in every child to receive the love of both parents.

After revealing to me the Father's words of affirmation to Jesus at His baptism, the Holy Ghost took me to the crucifixion when Jesus cried aloud, *"My God, my God, why has thou forsaken me?"* He spoke to me and said Jesus not only needed to hear and feel the Father's love and affirmation, but He was willing to experience God's rejection on the Cross so that I could be healed from my father's rejection. I don't know how long I was on my knees and cried tears of joy, but when I got up, I arose a new man. The Cross made me a new creation in Christ Jesus as it paid the price for my sins to be forgiven, but Pentecost enabled me to become a new person as the presence and power of the Holy Ghost comforts, teaches and lead and guide us into all truth.  He showed me the truth of Jesus relationship with Father God and the price He paid on Calvary so that me and every other person who suffers from the rejection of their father can look to Christ and be healed.

## CHAPTER THREE

---

*Beam In Your Eye*

---

There were things I felt in my heart about my son's mother that was never spoken. I don't believe it's our job to tell everything that we believe is wrong with our spouse or others for that matter. I felt strongly about certain things about her. One late night I was on my knees in my living room praying. I had asked God to show me my heart. My relationship with God was getting stronger, and I made this request to Father. In only what could be described as less than a moment, God allowed me to see my heart. It was quicker than the blink of an eye, yet what I saw was so wicked, dark and sinister it made me scream aloud at the top of my lungs! God doesn't just see all of us. He sees through us. I was reminded of Hebrews 12, The Word of God is quick (alive) and powerful and sharper than a double-edged sword, to the dividing asunder of soul and spirit, bones and marrow and the thoughts and intentions of the heart. Jeremiah 17:9 states *"the heart is deceitful above all things, and desperately wicked, who can know it."* I found out that evening the meaning of that scripture. At that moment I not only saw a glimpse of my heart, but God revealed to me intimately that the very things I believed and judged in my heart about my wife were actually deep inside of me. Jealousy, insecurity, wounded spirit, impatience, anger, pride. He showed me I'd been clinically depressed since my freshman year in high school and how that weak, emotionally fragile little boy was still living inside me. I don't know how long I wept and repented that night. I saw a speck in my wife's eye while a beam was in my own eye. There is absolutely nothing redeeming about judging others. The only person we can change is our self. Paul stated, *"Judge yourself to see if ye be in the faith."* 2 Corinthians 13:5

God is light. The closer we get to Him the more spots we will see on ourselves. He reveals them to heal and deliver us and give us more of Him. God cannot pour into filled vessels. We don't know how full of ourselves we are and it's the single most reason why so little of Him live inside us. The beginning of God is at the end of self. We are our worse enemy.

## Different Looks for Pride

Pride is insidious meaning, proceeding in a gradual, subtle way, but with harmful affects. Pride is the greatest chameleon and knows how to camouflage in any situation. The Bible speaks of the pride of life, a proud look, crown of pride, pride of heart, to name a few. Pride is easily detected in some while more elusive in others. We are born in sin and pride of life is one of the characteristics of the fallen nature. Most will never see and admit the sickness of pride living within us. The Spirit of God through the Word of God will be the agent to expose and close pride door in your life. Early on in my walk with God, in my immaturity, I asked some pretty stupid things about God and made some very bold promises to him. He is a loving Father and understands us better than we will ever know, but as I look back on a lot of what I said in my personal time with God, I realize how much pride was a stronghold in my heart. I remember the early 90's when many great leaders in the church were being exposed, like Jim Baker and Jimmy Swaggart. In my prayer time, I would tell God how I would never do the things they did. Being religious and arrogant is like wet with water. I was extremely religious and didn't realize it. There isn't anything on the planet more destructive, divisive, and degrading than religion. So many of us believe we love God and are doing His will when in fact, we are behaving the very opposite of His nature. Like Saul of Tarsus before he was changed into Paul the apostle, we use the scriptures to inflate our won self-righteousness as we go about judging and condemning others. My spiritual outlook was diseased and pride was the virus in my system. There are many things I would change or take back during those years. I see how many of my mistakes stemmed from the presence of pride in my heart. I'm so grateful that God doesn't leave us in our mess and sent Hs Spirit to teach us and transform us into the image of Jesus Christ.

---

*Pupil*

---

The pupil is the opening of the Iris of the eye. Pupil is also defined as a student. We must become pupils of our own pupil or students of the condition of our sight. When Adam and Eve ate from the forbidden tree, their eyes were opened, and they saw themselves. Since the fall we are born into this fallen world beholding all the wrong things including the number one enemy which is in-a-me; self. When we first come to the saving grace of Jesus Christ many of us immediately feel the urge to run and tell others about their faults and shortcomings. We believe this is honorable and that we are working for the Lord. Our zeal for God mixed with the lack of knowledge of His ways causes us to become the judge and jury for everyone around us. God will never use us to be our brother and sister's judge! He alone is Judge. Judgmentalism is a sickness inside every person. Life is always easier objectively than it is subjectively, meaning it seems to be so much easier to see others faults and know how to fix them than it is to see our faults and solve them. Becoming a pupil of our own pupil is one of the highest goals in life. The day, hour, and minute we lay down the judges gavel concerning others and judge no one else in life but the man in the mirror is the day God's heart is filled with joy knowing we have crossed over from being a hearer of His Word to a genuine doer of His Word. The greatest enemy we will ever face in this life is me, myself and I.

## It's not what you say

S unday night service had just ended at my church, and I was outside the sanctuary about to load my family in the car when my wife turned to go back into the vestibule of the church to get something. I called her name to get her attention. She came to see what I needed and returned to the church. An elder of the church I respected and was mentoring me called me. I walked up to him, and he pulled me to the side. He told me there was something he needed to talk to me about. He went on to tell me that the way I sometimes spoke to my wife was rude and disrespectful. He pointed out how my tone was demeaning. I was upset that he was in my business, but he was such a humble and nice man that I knew what he saw had to have some validity for him to pull me on the carpet so suddenly about it. Another part of me attempted to discount it as I said to myself, he must have a crush on my wife. In the end, I knew he was spot on. As I thought about what he said and realized what I said was never really a problem, but the body language and how I said things were the issue. My noncommunication skills were awful. Because we don't have mirrors in front of us during our interaction with others we never really get a chance to see what they see when we communicate with them. My tone of voice and body language was absolutely demeaning. That elder was one of the few men in my life who had the courage to call me out. I thank God for his backbone and leadership in my life.

## *90-10 Rule*

I went through a very emotionally bitter divorce. I spent a lot of my time contemplating all the ways my ex-failed and let me down until one day I was listening to a message from a pastor who stated something that changed the course of my thinking and helped me to move on. He stated concerning your spouse, *"They may be ninety percent of the problem, but your ten percent may trigger their ninety percent."* When I heard those words, it pricked the core of my heart. I knew two things at that moment. One, I may have only been a small degree of the problems of my marriage, but I was still not innocent and had a part to play in its demise. I understood wholeheartedly that my ten percent probably triggered their ninety percent especially since God created woman as reactionary beings. Women respond (negative or positive) to what men say or do. My quick temper and inability to compromise on anything I believed in had to be difficult to cope with. Secondly, no matter how much I fasted, prayed, spoke positive words, the only person I could change was myself. I called my ex and told her the revelation I received and asked for her forgiveness for my part in the death of our marriage. It did not subside the hurt, but it gave me the push that I needed to begin my journey to healing and recovery.

*Attitude determines Altitude*

My favorite t-shirt said, *"I Love My Attitude Problem."* When I saw the shirt in the store, my eyes lit up. It was as if someone heard my thoughts and made that shirt just for me. I was so arrogant and blind that I wore the t-shirt many times to church. That statement was my Anthem! As if to announce to all the fun-loving people in the world who felt the need to approach me and ask, *"what's the problem, it'll get better"* or *"smile; it can't be that bad."* They could read my thoughts on my chest before they made the fatal mistake of getting in my face. My aunt Loretta approached me after a Tuesday night service at church and began to prophesy to me. One of the words she gave me was that God said He loved me and was pleased with me. Words cannot express how much I needed to hear that from Father. When she finished telling me what God put on her heart she politely said, *"don't wear that shirt anymore."* I can't explain it except that at that moment a light came on and my eyes were open, and I realized for the first time how offensive and embarrassing the slogan was and how it had no business being displayed in God's house. I could not believe I was actually in love with that shirt and had the nerve to wear it to church. My walk to my car was a walk of shame, and it seemed like it took a year to make it out the church. I repented to God and threw the shirt away.

# CHAPTER FOUR

## *Unholy Trinity*

*Here is wisdom. Let him that hath understanding count the number of the beast: for it is the number of a man, and his number is Six hundred threescore and six.*

Revelation 13:18

The world is awaiting a mysterious "unholy trinity" to arise who is supposed to take the world by storm during the last days of this age. This "unholy trinity" will consist of the antichrist (first beast), the false prophet (second beast) and the image of the beast. Well, John said that the spirit of anti-Christ was already at work in his day (1 John 4:3). If it was at work in his day, it is definitely at work today. I believe we are born with this *"unholy trinity"* inside of us called, *"Me, Myself, and I."* Man is a tripartite being: one person consisting of three parts. Man is a *spirit,* with a *soul,* who lives in a *body.* The "unholy trinity" who is mentioned in the Book of Revelation is a picture of man's spirit, soul, and body in its fallen state.

Revelation 13:1 says that the first beast rose up out of the sea. Revelation 13:11 says that the second beast came up out the Earth. Water is symbolic of the Spirit. Jesus said we are born again of the water and of the Spirit. He related water to the Spirit. He told the Samaritan woman at Jacob's well that rivers of living water would flow from her belly. Jesus was referring to the Spirit of God. The first beast came up out of the sea because it was a picture of the origin of man's Spirit, man coming from the water of the Spirit.

The second beast came from the Earth because Genesis 2:7 says that God formed man from the dust of the Earth. Man's physical body originated from dirt. When a man dies, he returns to the dirt. The third person of this *"unholy trinity"* is called *"the image of the beast"* because he represents the soul of man. The soul houses man's mind, will, and emotions. This is where man imagines, thinks, and emotes. The "image of the beast" symbolizes man's soul, the place of images.  All three in this "unholy trinity" have beast in their names because on the same day (the sixth day) that God made man (of three parts), He also made the beast.  If man is three parts: spirit, soul, and body and God made him on the sixth day, then that is three (3) sixes (6's) he was made with 666.

Seven is the number of completion and perfection.  Six is one less than seven.  Therefore, no matter how brilliant, wise, or intelligent man becomes, he will always be one short of completion and perfection.  The number one is the number of God.  Israel declared, "The Lord our God, He is one."  This means that man (6) without God (1) will never fulfill his potential because God made man.  Six plus one equals seven and man plus God equals completion. Therefore, six will forever be fallen, short, and incapable. Stop looking for the revelation of the antichrist.  He is already here with his false prophet and the image of the beast living on the inside of you: "Me, Myself, and I."

Revelation Chapter Thirteen records that anyone who does not worship their image would be threatened with death. This points to the pride that is connected to each of us. We are born with an ungodly need to be catered for, adored, and worshipped. There is a beast in the waters of our Spirit. There is a beast in the imagination of our soul. And there is a beast in the dirt of our body. They are our worst enemies. They are the reason we do the evil and wickedness we do. As long as they stay in an unregenerate state, we will continue through life seeking our will, our way, and our selfish desires. Paul said, *"when I will to do good evil is present." Romans 7:21* This "unholy trinity" is the beam in our eye, the thorn in our flesh, and the constant itch in us to sin. The man of sin is you. The son of perdition and the antichrist is you because you are your greatest enemy.

Revelation 13:17 states there is a mark of the beast, name of the beast, and number of the beast. The mark of the beast is pride. The name of the beast is flesh (man), and the number of his name is 666. When we live life as if there is no God in Heaven and we do not have to answer to anyone, we have the mark of the beast. When we cannot see past our address, and nothing matters more than where we live, what we eat, and what we wear, we have the mark of the beast. When we examine our checkbook, and all of our finances went to meet our needs and purchase our pleasures, we have the mark of the beast. There is no need to look for a future "unholy trinity" who will control the world because they are living on the inside of us right now controlling our world and they are called: Me, Myself, and I.

## CHAPTER FIVE

---

## *Close our Eyes*

---

*And the eyes of them both were opened, and they knew that they were naked; and they sewed fig leaves together, and made themselves aprons.*

Genesis 3:7

The evidence that man had fallen after eating from the forbidden tree was that they saw themselves.  The first sign that you may be in error is usually when all you see is you.  Whenever we see the big "I," everyone else becomes a little "u."  Adam's and Eve's spiritual eyes were closed, and their physical eyes were opened.  When this occurred, they suddenly saw themselves for the first time.

When their eyes were opened, they saw "I." This is why we need to be born again because the born again part of us (spiritual) doesn't see us, but it sees Jesus. It sees the needs of others. It sees the will of God and not the will of man. The majority of our problems are rooted right here. The real enemy is in us, not outside of us. Man is born into this world self-centered, self-righteous, full of pride, and selfish. There is a sickness inside of everyone named, "self." Self-awareness was birthed in the Garden of Eden, and it is our greatest foe.

Christ is the Only Answer to this "disease" within each of us that causes us to see ourselves. The letter "I" is in the center of some pretty powerful words like pride, sin, and Lucifer. Whenever all you see, is you, expect a fall because the Word of God says that pride goes before destruction, and a haughty look before a fall (Proverbs 16:18). When our eyes see "I," we become blind to the hurts, needs, and wants of others. "I," is at the center of pride and it is consuming. You cannot serve "I" and others.

It is hard for us to comprehend that we are our worst enemy. It is intellectually and emotionally easier for us to see someone else as the villain. However, the truth of the matter is, the most degrading, poisonous, callous, lying, backstabbing, fornicating, unrighteous, wicked person you know is yourself. It is not until we accept this reality that we can even begin to understand and truly receive the forgiveness and grace that Jesus offers us through His sacrifice at Calvary. Humility says, "I am nothing!" Jesus said, "there is none good but God." When we can say from our hearts that we are not good, then we have dealt a crucial blow to the root of pride that resides deep on the inside of us.

Jesus taught us that our *old man of the flesh* must die. The life of peace, righteousness, and joy is a selfless lifestyle. When all of our energy is spent serving and pleasing self, we will never enjoy the true "abundant life." The secret to life is service. Whether it is marriage, business, or day-to-day living, serving others is the secret to real happiness and success. Serving yourself may reap temporary pleasure, but it will not last very long. God designed joy to overflow when we meet the needs of others, and not our own.

When Adam and Eve saw themselves, they immediately rushed to cover up. This is what we do, also. In our hearts, we know that the life of selfishness and pride is wrong. But instead of humbling ourselves to God, we run to cover our sin and arrogance with fig leaves of religion, false righteousness, dead works, and excuses. Exposure brings closure. The only way to deal with the pride of selfishness is through the transparency of humility. *1 Peter 5:6* says, "Humble yourselves therefore under the mighty hand of God, that he may exalt you in due time." It is against our fallen nature to desire nakedness or total transparency before God and man. We do not want others to see and know our secret sins, our hidden faults, our scars, and flaws. On the contrary, these areas in our lives cannot be healed and made whole until we first expose them. God does not desire us to reveal them to hurt us, but He desires total exposure so we can be liberated.

*Exposure brings closure*

The man with the withered hand that Jesus healed on the Sabbath day had to deal with this reality. In Jewish tradition, the right and left hand had distinct purposes. The left hand was the private hand, and the right hand was the public hand. The left hand stayed hidden within one's robe, and it was used exclusively for hygienic purposes like washing up. The right hand was always exposed, and it was used for things like greeting and shaking others' hands. This particular man's right hand was withered. This made him feel accursed, embarrassed, and ashamed because he could not salute his neighbor, shake hands, or hug.

Jesus understood his pain and knew what He was doing when He commanded this man to stretch forth his hand. He asked him to do this publicly because his shame was public. It was bad enough the man couldn't use his right hand. Now, Jesus wanted him to show the ugliness of his hand. Pride would have kept this man from his healing. Pride tells us never to expose our pain and suffering. Pride begs us to never unveil the true source of our feelings of inferiority and condemnation. But some things must be done publicly. Usually, the greater the deliverance we need, the greater the humility will be required to get it. Humility is the absence of self. Humility is the death of pride. It is the only path to life. When the man with the withered hand humbled himself and trusted Jesus enough to reveal his worst flaw, he was healed and restored to a life without shame and guilt.

When all you see is you, know that you have already fallen. The nature of Christ is the opposite of pride. Matthew 10:39 says, *"He that findeth his life shall lose it: and he that loseth his life for my sake shall find it."* We've been looking from the supercilious eyes of the flesh too long. These selfish eyes were opened by Adam and Eve and can only be closed by trusting in Jesus. We had no control over being born with the type of sight that is proud and self-centered, but we do have control over choosing to be born again and living life through the selfless eyes of the Spirit.

Adam and Eve hid from the Presence of God. No proud person desires to be close to God because God is the very opposite of that spirit. Humility is the death of that haughty nature. Humility automatically causes us to become closer to God. Sin makes us run from God and righteousness makes us run to God. Two objects cannot occupy the same space at the same time. We cannot live lives of arrogance and desire God's Presence. They are contrary, one to another. When we deal with the real enemy inside of us, that is the pride of life and reckon him as dead like the Bible instructs us, then we will not have any guilty feelings about approaching the Presence of God.

The institution of marriage has become a joke because of our pride. We cannot be pleased. Consequently, when we can't seem to please us, we hurry up and leave. We must do something with the eyes that only see "I." The "I" must die. Paul said, *"...nevertheless I live; yet not I, but Christ liveth in me." Galatians 2:20* He also said, *"I die daily." 1 Corinthians 15:31b*  The eyes of the flesh that only see "I" must die daily.  "I" is also the center letter in "die."  When we are in "I," we sin.  The day that we sin, we shall surely die.

## CHAPTER SIX

---

## *Lead While You Bleed*

---

*Therefore I take pleasure in infirmities, in reproaches, in necessities, in persecutions, in distresses for Christ's sake: for when I am weak, then am I strong.*

2 Corinthians 12:10

There is a "gospel" being preached today that is false, watered down, or at best, ignorant. You would be surprised what you would find if you looked up certain words in the New Testament like glory, blessed, and pleasure. We would agree that these words seem to be very positive and encouraging, but a little studying will reveal that God's definitions are not ours.

In the above Scripture, Paul said that he took pleasure in things that none of us would consider pleasurable. *Infirmities* is the Greek word *astheneia* meaning, *feebleness (of body or mind), malady, frailty, disease, sickness,* and *weakness. Reproaches* is the Greek word *hubris* meaning, *insult, injury, harm,* and *hurt. Necessities* is the Greek word *anagke* meaning, *distress, must need,* and *needful. Distresses* is the Greek word *stenochoria* meaning, the *narrowness of room, calamity, anguish,* and *distress.*

Can you say you take pleasure when you feel feeble, frail, diseased, sick, and weak? Do you feel satisfied when others insult you, injure, and harm you? Do you get immediate relief when times are distressing, calamity hits you, and anguish is all around you? Well, Paul got to a place in his walk with God that this became his reality because he understood that he was not saved to sit. He understood that on this side of Glory, the Kingdom he was called to represent would attract attack. Today we hear a lot concerning prosperity, wealth, and increase. Is it just me or have we forgotten about the word "suffering?"

These are the words of Jesus concerning the call of the Apostle Paul:

*For I will shew him how great things he must suffer for my name's sake.*

Acts 9:16

Paul's sufferings never stopped his progress, but it fueled it. Some people break under pressure, but Children of the Kingdom are supposed to focus and become a greater threat to the enemy when under pressure because it is the pressure that squeezes the glory, power, and nature of Christ out of us. We do not know what is in us until we are squeezed the right way. Some people curse when they are squeezed, and some people pray. We must understand that pain is our partner. It is designed to bring out the best in us and bury the worst in us. Muscle is not built strictly from the presence of weight, but it is built when we resist the weight and push the weight back. *"Resist the devil, and he will flee from you."* James 4:7b Each time we say, "no" to the weight of the pleasure of sin and selfishness, we are pushing it back and building stronger spiritual muscles.

God knows that our greatest enemy is ourselves. Therefore, He orchestrates each battle to be waged right in our face. We cannot grasp just how messed up we are and how much internal purging we need. Since the Fall gave life to death, the only cure is to give death to our self-life. The lust of the eyes, the lust of the flesh and the pride of life are the three areas we must overcome daily. Suffering is the prescription given, to cleanse us from these three areas.

*God's glory*

*As Believer's we desire the Glory of God. However, if we look at Scripture, we will find that God's Glory is always connected to sufferings.*

*For I reckon that the sufferings of this present time are not worthy to be compared with the glory which shall be revealed in us.*

Romans 8:18

*For our light affliction, which is but for a moment, worketh for us a far more exceeding and eternal weight of glory.*

2 Corinthians 4:17

We see from these two Scriptures that God's Glory being revealed in us is directly connected to our sufferings. To have God's glory manifested in our lives, it will take the key of suffering to unlock it. Right after Judas left from the Last Supper to betray Jesus, the Lord had these words to say in John 13:31, *"Now is the Son of man glorified, and God is glorified in him."* Jesus never said that He was glorified until it was time to die. They left the Upper Room and went straight to the Garden of Gethsemane where He began to travail knowing the cross was before Him. While praying there, something interesting was said by the Lord, *"...not my will, but thine, be done."* Jesus revealed that for the first time since Eternity Past; He had a will, different than the Father's.

---

### *Not my will*

---

It is our wills that cause many of our problems.  Lucifer said in his heart, "*I will* ascend into heaven, *I will* exalt my throne above the stars of God: *I will* also sit upon the mount of the congregation . . . , *I will* ascend above the heights of the clouds; *I will* be like the most High." *Isaiah 14:13-14*  Christ Jesus said, *"Except a corn of wheat fall into the ground and die, it abideth alone..."* John 12:24 satan always appeals to the lower nature, that is high-minded and the Lord always appeal to the higher nature, that is humble-minded.  Before Jesus ascended, He first descended.  The way up is down!

In Gethsemane, Christ prayed the most powerful prayer when He said, *"...not my will, but thine be done."* Luke 22:42 When we continue to resist God's will, this is where much of our sufferings come into play.  Dying to self means the closing of the selfish eyes that were opened in the Garden of Eden.  Taking up your cross and following

Jesus is the crucifixion of our "I will."  If we don't suffer with Jesus, we cannot reign with Him.  Philippians Chapter Two says that Jesus made Himself of no reputation and humbled Himself and became obedient even unto death (*Philippians 2:6-8*).  There is an "unholy trinity" living on the inside of us who desires to have a reputation.  He longs for his way and desires his way to be executed.  His greatest fear is that one day he will die and he will not be able to control us through pride, guilt, shame, condemnation, lust, and his many vices.

Jesus was obedient unto death, and we must be obedient unto death, also.  In this life, we are not strong until we are weak.  As long as we focus on our gifts, talents, intelligence, bank account, beauty, and earthly wisdom, we will fall again and again.  It is in our weakness that God's strength is made perfect.  God's beginning is at our end.  As long as our eyes are open and we see ourselves, as long as "John" is a voice crying in our wilderness, and as long as we are like Lucifer saying in our hearts, "I will," we will stay limited and defeated in our Christian walk.  Life doesn't begin until we surrender our lives to God.

Instead of getting upset each time something or someone gets under your skin, look at it like Apostle Paul and say, *"I will take pleasure in my infirmities . . ."* Don't take it personal, but see it as an opportunity to die to self. Jesus said, *"Blessed are ye, when men shall revile you, and persecute you." Matthew 5:11a* Use every "thorn in the flesh," every uncomfortable situation, and every offended feeling as an occasion to deny yourself and bury "Me, Myself, and I" six feet under where he belongs.

God's Army is not like man's army. When you are injured in man's army, you get to go home. In God's Army, the battle doesn't even get started until you are wounded, offended, or hurt. As long as you are wounded, you are weak. As long as you are limping, you are humble. God can use this weakness in us as an open door to show Himself strong.

We have to learn how to "lead while we bleed." Life has many twists and turns. It consists of seasons with many different climates and atmospheres. Many times, it can seem very unpredictable. But the Saints are supposed to be as bold as lions. We must still fight even though we've been through a divorce. We still have to move forward even when life has seemed to set us back. We must continue to pray for healing for the sick though we are diseased. Although we feel bound, we cannot stop visiting the prisoners. We walk by faith and not by sight. The world doesn't need another "fair-weather" Christian. The world needs true sons of God. A true son of God will, *"...deny himself, and take up his cross,"* and follow Christ. *Matthew 16:24*

We have rewards waiting for us on the other side that is unfathomable. There are colors our human eye cannot see. There are sounds and emotions that our natural tongue cannot begin to explain. In this life, we are called to die to live. We are to endure hardness as a good soldier (*2 Timothy 2:3*) and die to this world every day we awaken. The Bible says that we will receive rewards for our good done in this life. You don't want the fleeting, temporal five minutes of fame man has to offer for your works of labor. You want to do God's will in the closet so He can reward you openly. Don't sell your birthright to newspapers, articles, and carnal award ceremonies. Wait to stand in the palatial halls of Heaven with myriads of angels flanked in every direction and the Universe standing at attention as the God of Heaven and Earth announce every sacrificial work done by you. You want to wait for all of Creation to witness the reception of your crowns, jewels, and medals of honor. What can compare to the Lord Himself saying, *"Well done, thou good and faithful servant: thou hast been faithful...enter thou into the joy of thy lord." Matthew 25:21* You will then throw your crowns down at His feet and bow down saying, "Holy, Holy, Holy, is the Lord God Almighty," because you understand that it was Christ empowering you to do the things you did,  If you really think about it, we aren't losing anything, but we are gaining everything. Let your prayer be, *"Lord I am nothing, that You may be Everything. Today, deliver me from "Me, Myself, and I."*

CHAPTER SEVEN

---

*Humility*

---

**Before destruction the heart of man is haughty, and before honour is humility.**

Proverbs 18:12

We've gone into great detail to diagnose and explain the pride of man and its destructive effects. Now let's talk about the antidote to Satan's greatest disease planted inside of mankind. The only antidote to pride and selfishness is humility. Humility can be defined as the total emptying of oneself and total dependency on God for everything. Humility is the death of self and an absolute, desperate need for God's life. It is when we realize that self has nothing good in it. Then, we can bring ourselves before God empty, so He can help us. We must get the revelation that we lose nothing by giving God everything.

Whatever you call "normal," you are not able to change. As long as you are comfortable with being self-centered and looking out for no one but "Me, Myself, and I," you will never be able to take the necessary steps to change your behavior and become more like Christ. Death is the only pathway to life. Jesus said in *Matthew 16: 24-26*:

*. . . If any man will come after me, let him deny himself, and take up his cross, and follow me.*

*For whosoever will save his life shall lose it: and whosoever will lose his life for my sake shall find it.*

*For what is a man profited, if he shall gain the whole world, and lose his own soul? Or what shall a man give in exchange for his soul?*

When we are able to humble ourselves before God, we will be able to humble ourselves before man. The only way to prove your humility towards God Who you cannot see is by loving and serving man who you can see. All the commandments hang on these two commandments, *"...love the Lord thy God with all thy heart, and with all thy soul, and with all thy mind, and with all thy strength...love thy neighbor as thyself." Mark 12:30-31* This is why the Cross was both horizontal and vertical because our love towards God can only be authenticated by our love towards man.

---

*Dying to live*

---

We must first be aware of the many ways we attempt to save our lives. Saving our lives comes in many different forms. For example, when dinner is served, and you hurry up to grab the plate with the most food on it, you saved your life. When you are down to one piece of gum, and you refuse to give it to your friend, you just saved your life. When you just climbed up all the stairs, then someone asks you to go downstairs to get them a glass of water, and you give them an excuse, you saved your life. When you continue to drive past people needing assistance on the side of the road, or only buy gifts for those with the same last name, or only do good for others when you know a nice thank you will be returned, you saved your life.

We must lay our hearts on the altar of God's Word and allow the Spirit of God to perform heart surgery. On our best day, we are wicked. On our greatest day, we are fallen. We must surrender and ask the Lord for His grace to live a crucified life before Him. Jesus said, *"deny yourself"* (*Matthew 16:24*). We find that to be the hardest task on the planet. How does one deny his very nature and desire to always be the first? Through blood, sweat, and tears, that's how. When it was time for Jesus to die for our sins, it was no walk in the park. Before the soldiers showed up in the Garden of Gethsemane, Jesus had already prayed three times and was in so much pain and travail that He was sweating great drops of Blood. No one said it would be easy, but God always makes it worth it.

---

*Humble yourself*

---

Somebody lied and told us once we give our hearts to God everything gets easier. They said that God would begin to bless us with bigger houses, cars, and financial wealth. That is the Magic Kingdom. It is not God's Kingdom. True followers of Christ suffer. Not through sickness and disease and constant defeat, but we suffer daily because we choose to take the low road that is really the high road. We choose to consider our brother above ourselves. We choose to get out of our comfort zone in order to help someone else. We choose to sacrifice our will to help further God's will on Earth. We do this by denying ourselves. We deny the pleasures of this world. In order to see others come into eternal life, deny yourself a full belly of food while you fast and pray for your city to have Revival. Deny yourself a few worldly amenities to help give to missions and organizations that feed the hungry. Deny yourself sleep so that God can reveal some hidden things to you in His word. We are constantly losing our lives so that we can gain it.

The Word says, *"Humble yourselves therefore under the mighty hand of God, that he may exalt you in due time."* 1 Peter 5:6  God is a just God.  He is not asking us to give everything and be left with no reward, but His reward may not be your reward.  When He exalts us, it isn't necessarily a bigger ministry, monetary riches, position, status, power, fame, and fortune.  The way God exalts us has been the same from the beginning; He gives us more of Himself.  God told Abraham, *"I am thy shield, and thy exceeding great reward."* Genesis 15:1

What is more priceless than God?  When we humble ourselves before Him, He gives us more of His nature, His person, and His ways.  What could be more valuable than one drop of God, a pinch of unconditional love, an ounce of eternity, a milliliter of mercy, a nanogram of compassion, a glance at His face, a speck of longsuffering, a crumb of His loving-kindness, an echo of His Voice, or one Word from Father?  King David said, *"One thing have I desired of the Lord, that will I seek after; that I may dwell in the house of the Lord all the days of my life."* Psalm 27:4 Our problem is that God isn't the "One Thing" Who we desire. Our hearts are still set on earthly things, not on heavenly things. As a result of our hearts being focused on earthly things, we are easily seduced and filled with wrong desires. God has always yearned to not only be first in our lives but the Only One in our lives!

Jesus said, *"...for without me ye can do nothing."* John 15:5 We hear these words, but we don't believe them. When push comes to shove, we still run to our credit score, last name, friends, and family, savings and investments, financial institutions, or the mercy of others. Why is it that we do not call on God for His help until we have exhausted every other feasible avenue? It is because we don't believe that without Him we could do nothing. We must learn to depend on God for our socks. We must depend on Him for our daily bread. We can lose jobs, spouses, careers, and friends. However, He will never leave us nor forsake us (*Hebrews 13:5*). Humility is depending on the Lord for everything.

## *Sold out*

Humility is also being sold out.  Have you ever went to the movies and when you asked for tickets for a certain show, the cashier told you they were sold out?  What they meant was that there was no more room left in the theatre for that showing. Christians today are not sold out!  We still have room inside of us for more lust, more strife, and more of the world.  Yet, when you are sold out for Jesus, you have no more room for that stuff.  Jesus said, *"...for the prince of this world cometh, and hath nothing in me."* John 14:30 Can we say when the enemy comes he will not have anything in us?  If you are sold out you can.  If you are dead you can.  A dead man doesn't have a will.  A dead man can't get offended.  A dead man doesn't defend himself.  A dead man doesn't need to justify himself.  The Bible says, *"...reckon ye also yourselves to be dead indeed unto sin."* Romans 6:11  Humility is the only pathway to death, and this death brings life.  When we are dead, God is alive and at work in us.  Trying to save the trifling life we are living is futile. Each time we save it, we actually lose it. There are peace and joy available, but it will never be found while attempting to serve "Me, Myself, and I."

Jesus is our greatest Example of humility. He is Almighty God Who chose to come through Mary's virgin womb in order to look like us, talk like us, and feel like us. It is impossible for us to comprehend this because we do not have any idea what it is like to be Omnipresent, Omnipotent, and Omniscient. Therefore, we can't understand the degree that Christ abased Himself when He was made flesh. In addition to de-robing Himself of His full Glory, as a man, He was the epitome of what it is to be humble. *Matthew 11:29-30* says:

*Take my yoke upon you, and learn of me; for I am meek and lowly in heart: and ye shall find rest unto your souls.*

*For my yoke is easy, and my burden is light.*

The Lord said that He was meek and lowly in heart and that we should learn of Him. The greater authority we have, the more humility is required, to lead according to

God's standard. Jesus said that if you desire to be first, you have to become the least because the first shall be last and the last shall be first (*Matthew 20:16, 26*). The world's standard for leadership is having more people under you to serve you, but that is not how the Kingdom of Heaven operates. The greatest are the least, and the least are the greatest.

The way we learn from Christ is by looking at the example He left us. The King of the Universe got down on His knees and washed His twelve disciples feet, knowing that one of them was about to betray him. Afterwards, He commanded them to do the same to one another. He didn't choose to be born in royalty under the guard of legions, tucked away comfortably in some magnificent castle. But God was born in the lowliest of all places, a germ-infested, stinking manger surrounded by common animals.

Wherever there is pride, satan has a doorway. Pride is cunning and subtle, and we must always be aware of its presence. Pride needs to be heard. It has to be seen, and it must be recognized. Can you help someone without being thanked?  Can you bless someone you do not know and expect nothing in return?  Can you do something extraordinary and stay ordinary?  Can you be like David who killed the giant Goliath and immediately went back to shepherding his father's smelly sheep?  Can you be like Jesus who miraculously feed thousands then hid away to be alone with God?

We become erudite when we get a couple of initials in front of our names.  For some, it can be the company's uniform on our back, being known by owning a certain business, or having a certain last name.  Whatever it is that fuels the spirit of self-importance, it must be dealt with swiftly.  Pride can never be allowed to linger, not even for a moment because all it takes is a moment to fall.  That moment becomes a seed that can reap a terrible harvest.

There is a story about a young minister who accepted his call into ministry.  This particular Sunday was his day to preach for the first time.  He had studied all night, prepared intricate notes, and felt secure and prepared to show everyone that he was going to be the next great preacher.   As the pastor introduced him to speak, he walked up the stairs with his shoulders broad and his head lifted high knowing he had the talent to do the job.  After stumbling over his words and forgetting some key points, he felt utter humiliation as he concluded.  He then walked slowly down the stairs with his head bowed.   After service, the senior pastor told him, *"If you had gone up the stairs the way you came down the stairs, you would have done fine."*

We have to avoid every opportunity to be puffed up. Humility is a conscious decision that becomes a condition of the heart.  There are times when God uses me to save many souls and there is always a voice on the inside that wants to be recognized and get a pat on the back, but I simply give God all the glory for what has occurred, go home, and go back to normal.  We must flee every occasion of vanity and self-gratification.  As long as we remain nothing, God will remain Everything.  As long as we stay empty, God can keep us filled.  Let's look at a few Scriptures concerning humility:

*But he giveth more grace.  Wherefore he saith, God resisteth the proud, but giveth grace unto the humble.*

James 4:6

*Put on therefore, as the elect of God, holy and beloved, bowels of mercies, kindness, humbleness of mind, meekness, longsuffering;*

*forbearing one another, and forgiving one another, if any man have a quarrel against any: even as Christ forgave you, so also do ye.*

*And above all these things put on charity, which is the bond of perfectness.*

Colossians 3:12-14

*Likewise, ye younger, submit yourselves unto the elder.  Yea, all of you be subject one to another, and be clothed with humility: for God resisteth the proud, and giveth grace to the humble.*

*Humble yourselves therefore under the mighty hand of God, that he may exalt you in due time.*

1 Peter 5:5-6

*Better it is to be of an humble spirit with the lowly, than to divide the spoil with the proud.*

Proverbs 16:19

We are sealed with the Holy Spirit until the day of redemption. The day of redemption is when we look like, act like, and sound like our Lord and Savior Jesus Christ. Purpose in your heart to judge no one after the flesh and ask God's Spirit to help you be a more sensitive and compassionate person to those you encounter. When our greatest goal in life is to conquer the man in the mirror, we will no longer have time to worry about everyone else. Philippians 2: 12-13 says it best.

*Wherefore my beloved, as ye have always obeyed, not as in my presence only, but now much more in my absence, work out your own salvation with fear and trembling.*

*For it is God which worketh in you both to will and to do of his good pleasure.*

# *Prayer of Salvation*

Heavenly Father, I admit I am a sinner in need of a Savior. I repent of all my sins, and I believe based on Romans chapter ten that if I confess with my mouth the Lord Jesus and believe in my heart that you Father, raised Jesus from the dead, I will be saved. You said you would cast my sins into the lake of forgetfulness and remember them no more. Thank you for saving me and cleansing me from all unrighteousness. In Jesus name, I pray.

# About the Author

Over 25 years, Romel Duane Moore Sr has penned many profound insights on the Word of God. He credits every revelation as the fruit of maintaining a sacred relationship with the Holy Spirit. The books that he publishes are done so in obedience to the calling that the Lord has bestowed upon him. A gift that he honors greatly, Romel is committed to present the message of the Gospel of Jesus Christ as the scarlet thread that God has woven into scripture and connects its reappearance all throughout the Bible. It is his prayer that every reader becomes a believer with a newfound reverence for the written Word of God. All of Romel's books are available on Amazon and Kindle. If you desire to contact Romel for speaking engagements you may reach him at (808) 397-4906.

# *Footnotes*

[1] **infirmities.** The New Strong's Expanded Exhaustive Concordance of the Bible, Copyright © 2001 by Thomas Nelson Publishers. Published in Nashville, TN, by Thomas Nelson, Inc., Greek word #769 *astheneia* meaning, *feebleness (of body or mind), malady, frailty, weakness, diseases,* and *sickness*. This word literally means *lacking strength, weakness,* and *infirmity* and is translated *weakness* in this Scripture text. This Greek word comes from #772.

[2] **reproaches.** The New Strong's Expanded Exhaustive Concordance of the Bible, Copyright © 2001 by Thomas Nelson Publishers. Published in Nashville, TN, by Thomas Nelson, Inc., Greek word #5196 *hubris* meaning *insolence (as over-bearing) that is insult, injury, harm, hurt* and *reproach*. Hubris denotes *reproaches* (*more than reproach is conveyed by the term*). This Greek word is from #5228.

[3] **necessities.** The New Strong's Expanded Exhaustive Concordance of the Bible, Copyright © 2001 by Thomas Nelson Publishers. Published in Nashville, TN, by Thomas Nelson, Inc., Greek word #318 *anagke* meaning

constraint, distress, must needs, and needful, etc. Anagke denotes *a necessity imposed whether by external circumstances or inward pressure.* This Greek word is from #303 and the base of #43.

[4] **distresses.** The New Strong's Expanded Exhaustive Concordance of the Bible, Copyright © 2001 by Thomas Nelson Publishers. Published in Nashville, TN, by Thomas Nelson, Inc., Greek word #4730 *stenochoria* meaning the *narrowness of room, calamity, anguish,* and *distress.* This Greek word is from a compound of #4728 and #5561.